CROSS-CULTURAL REVIEW #4

"South Korean Poets of Resistance"

한국의 저항시선

Compiled and Translated by Ko Won
Gouaches by Kang Sin Suk

고 원 편역

강신석 그림

Series Editor: Stanley H. Barkan

Cross-Cultural Communications
Merrick, New York
1980

Copyright © 1980 by Cross-Cultural Communications
Korean originals and art work Copyright © 1980 by the authors and the artist
English translations Copyright © 1980 by Ko Won

All rights reserved under International Copyright Conventions. Except for brief passages quoted in a newspaper, magazine, radio, or television review, no part of this book may be reproduced in any form or by any means, electronic or mechanical, including photocopying and recording, or by any information storage and retrieval system, without permission in writing from the publisher.

We are grateful to the Coordinating Council of Literary Magazines and the New York State Council on the Arts whose generous grant has made this publication possible.

Acknowledgment is also due, with thanks, to the editors of *Pulp* and *The Korean Review* who first published some of the translations of Kim Chi-ha and Yang Sŏng-u which are included in this volume.

CCR is a generally bilingual international journal of literature and art in *book format*, focusing on cultures in contact. The traditionally neglected languages and cultures are our primary concern. We anticipate six-twelve issues per year, each concentrating on a different geo-lingual group with particular emphasis on poetry, fiction, drama, and cross-cultural events, such as international poetry festivals, and also including graphics, interviews, cinematography, music, paintings, sculpture, and the dance. Specialists in these fields with an expertise in translation (where appropriate) are welcome to submit query letters. Submissions of individual works are limited to occasional English-only and/or mixed-translation issues; the latter should include the original-language version. All submissions should be in standard manuscript form; S.A.S.E. required for return of materials. All rights in copy matter will be treated as unconditionally assigned for publication to **CCR**, though copyright reverts to authors, translators, and artists upon publication.

Subscriptions: Individual: 6 issues/$24.00 (paper), $60.00 (cloth). Institutional & Foreign: 6 issues/$28.00 (paper), $65.00 (cloth). Postpaid. Single copies: $4.00 (paper), $10.00 (cloth). Postage & Handling: .75 U.S.A., $1.25 abroad. N.Y. residents add 8% sales tax.

Make checks payable and mail all correspondence to the publisher: **Cross-Cultural Communications,** 239 Wynsum Avenue, Merrick, N.Y. 11566/U.S.A. Telephone: (516) 868-5635.

Series Editor: Stanley H. Barkan. *Associate Editor:* Eva Feiler. *Art Editor:* Bebe Barkan. *Editorial Board:* David B. Axelrod, Joseph Bruchac, Edward Butscher, Roy Cravzow, Danica Cvetanovska, Enid Dame, Arthur Dobrin, Talat S. Halman, Leo Hamalian, J. C. Hand, Gunnar Harding, Ko Won, Aaron Kramer, Donald Lev, Ifeanyi A. Menkiti, Branko Mikasinovich, Anne Paolucci, Raymond R. Patterson, Nat Scammacca, Boris Vishinski, Hans van de Waarsenburg, Joost de Wit.

First Edition
Library of Congress Catalog Card Number: 79-90037
ISSN 0271-6186
ISBN 0-89304-606-X Clothbound
ISBN 0-89304-607-8 Paperbook
Designed by Bebe Barkan
Printed in the United States of America

CONTENTS

Foreword by Ko Won/ 고 원 4
KIM CHI-HA/김지하 7
황톳길 /The Yellow Dust Road 8
푸른 옷 /Blue Suit 12
아무도 없다 /Nobody Is There 14
서 울 /Seoul 16
YANG SŎNG-U/양성우 19
새 /Birds 20
겨울공화국 /The Winter Republic 22
夏日有感 /On a Summer Day 28
KO ŬN/고 은 31
푸른 하늘 /The Blue Sky 32
화 살 /Arrows 34
고 향 /Home 36
KO WON/고 원 39
탈상의 날에 /Going Out of Mourning 40
어머니 /Mother 42
아직도 숨을 쉰다면 /If You Are Still Breathing 46
About the Artist: Kang Sin Suk/강신석 48

GOUACHES by KANG SIN SUK
*(created especially for this volume
with thoughts of his son in Seoul)*
그림 • 강신석

"No. 10" (1980) .... Front Cover
"No. 11" (1980) 6
"No. 12" (1980) 18
"No. 13" (1980) 30
"No. 14" (1980) 38

FOREWORD

The writing of poetry in South Korea has become a political martyrdom for socially oriented poets since 1970, at latest, when Kim Chi-ha was arrested on the charge of having violated the so-called "Anti-Communist Law" for his long poem "Five Bandits," published in the *Sasanggye,* a monthly magazine. A few other poets joined Kim as prisoners of the Park Chung Hee regime: among them, Chang Ki-p'yo, the author of "Cry of the People" which first appeared anonymously in Japan in 1974; Kim Myŏng-sik, who is currently serving a five-year sentence for a poem entitled "10 Chapters of History"; and Moon Ik-hwan, a renowned Christian minister, who was released after Park's assassination and, soon re-arrested, is now on trial by the Chun Doo Hwan military regime under its full martial law.

It is obvious that the dictatorship practiced in South Korea is obsessed with its fear of poetry and the poet. That is to say, poetry is functioning as a vital force of expressing the people's mind, spirit, and life. The vein of satirical realism which began to flourish by younger poets in the 1960's has developed into a much more directly critical, activist type of engagement from the seventies on. The compiler-translator of this anthology, which was originally prepared early in 1979, has chosen to present four South Korean poets of resistance and sociopolitical consciousness: Kim Chi-ha in jail; Yang Sŏng-u who was released from prison toward the end of the Park regime; Ko Ŭn, currently standing military trial along with others; the compiler himself who, residing in the United States, supports their struggle.

The selection of the poets and their poems is not necessarily meant to represent "the best"; rather, it is made in terms of an exemplification of the different circumstances under which each poet is preoccupied with changing the threatening systems for the people of Korea. The compiler-translator's apologies are due to those who are not included here because of the space limit. Most of these poems have been written/published in Korean after 1970, and some of the English translations have appeared in American publications in the past few years. All the personal names are put in the Korean manner with the surname coming first: for instance, Kim Chi-ha instead of Chi-ha Kim.

There are a large number of "dissident" men of letters—published, unpublished, or anonymous—both in South Korea and abroad, not to mention the innumerable political prisoners, "prisoners of conscience," and impoverished, dehumanized, and, thus, fighting people against suppression and injustice. All of them unrelentingly resist South Korea's consecutive murderous regimes, dictatorships which oppose any attempt to reunify divided Korea.

Any sensible man and woman of good faith may find universal problems and meanings which are intensified in the poems of this collection.

Should the poet not be involved with politics? Should the sword of tyrannical power be allowed to subdue the marvel of poetic power? Should poetic imagination and poetic reality be divorced from political imagination and political reality? It seems that, in a suffering and struggling society like South Korea, "pure" or "independent" aesthetics of art for art's sake can hardly justify itself. The human, social, and political conditions there stir up, naturally, a new artistic impulse which requires its own style, perhaps beyond a conventional sort of labeling. Also, the unfinished quality of writing in many cases, aside from powerfulness, appears to be inevitable; the specific reality is often too harsh and immediate for the poet to polish or even complete his work. However, it is the translator who ought to take the blame for defects.

New York, 1980   *—Ko Won*

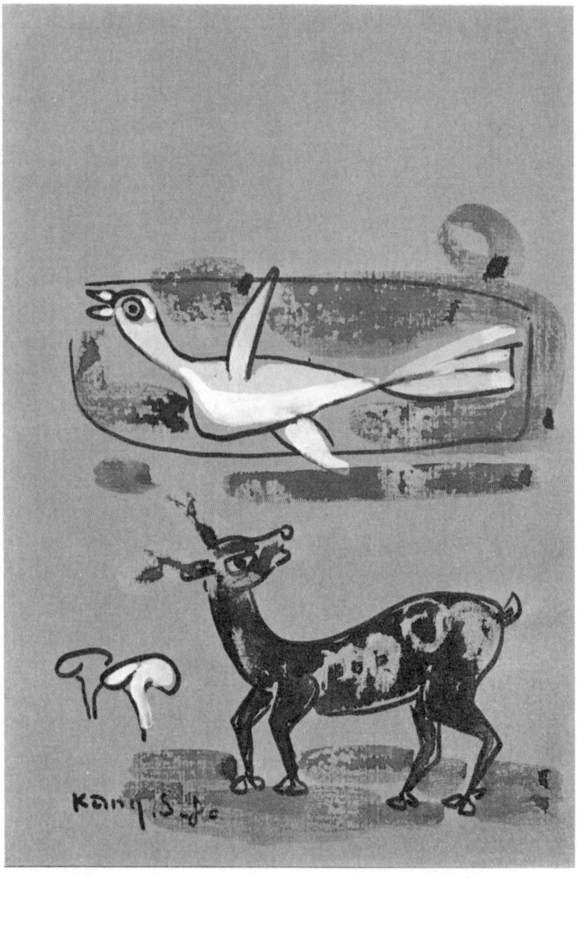

KIM CHI-HA
(b. 1941)

A symbol of the oppressed South Korean people's suffering and resistance, Kim Chi-ha (Kim Chi Ha, Kim Chiha), while he was studying aesthetics at Seoul National University, began to participate in political activities such as the much-opposed Korea-Japan normalization in 1964. He was arrested in 1970 on the charge of having violated the "Anti-Communist Law" immediately after his long poem (a ballad) "Ojŏk" (Five Bandits) had been published. Ever since, he was repeatedly rearrested with short intervals. In July 1974, a military tribunal of the Park regime sentenced him to death, but the sentence was later commuted to life imprisonment. Thanks to international pressures, he was released under a conditional amnesty in 1975—only, however, to be re-arrested in 27 days because of the publication of a newspaper series in which he exposed the fabrication of the so-called People's Revolutionary Party conspiracy.

Aside from his first book of poetry, *Hwangt'o* (The Yellow Dust Road, 1970), all other books in Korean have been published outside of Korea: *Kim Chi-ha sijip* (Poems of Kim Chi-ha, West Germany, 1975); *Kim Chi-ha chŏnjip* (Complete Works of Kim Chi-ha, Tokyo, 1975). Besides Japanese translations in book form, the English versions of Kim's poetry, plays, and other works include three books: *Cry of the People and Other Poems* (Hayama, Japan, 1974), *The Gold-Crowned Jesus and Other Writings* (Maryknoll, N.Y., 1978), and *The Middle Hour* (Stanfordville, N.Y., 1980). In June 1975, the Afro-Asian Writers Association awarded Kim its special Lotus Prize.

KIM CHI-HA／김지하

황톳길

황톳길에 선연한
핏자욱 핏자욱 따라
나는 간다 애비야
네가 죽었고
지금은 검고 해만 타는 곳
두 손엔 철삿줄
뜨거운 해가
땀과 눈물과 모밀밭을 태우는
총부리 칼날 아래 더위 속으로
나는 간다 애비야
네가 죽은 곳
부줏머리 갯가에 숭어가 뛸 때
가마니 속에서 네가 죽은 곳

밤마다 오포산에 불이 오를 때
울타리 탱자도 서슬푸른 속니파리
뻘시디 뻘친 성장처럼 억세인
황토에 대낮 빛나던 그날
그날의 만세라도 부르랴
노래라도 부르랴

대샆에 대가 성긴 동그만 화당골
우물마다 십년마다 피가 솟아도
아아 척박한 식민지에 태어나
총칼 아래 쓰러져간 나의 애비야
어이 죽순에 괴는 물방울
수정처럼 맑은 오월을 모르리 모르리마는

고 원 /KO WON

THE YELLOW DUST ROAD

Following the vivid marks of blood,
bloody marks on the yellow dust road,
I am going, Father,
where you died,
land now blackened, only the sun scorching.
With barbed wires in my hands,
rushing into the heat under the bayonets,
the hot sun burning up
sweat and tears and buckwheat paddies,
I am going, Father,
where you died,
where you died, indeed, wrapped in a rice sack
while the trouts were jumping along Pujutmŏri Brook.

Remember the day
when the blaze rose from Op'o Hill every night
whereas the bright sun shone on the yellow dust land
with the gorse on the fence growing fearless and fierce.
Shall we cry out the call of that day?
Shall we sing out the song of that day?

Born in the barren colony
while blood springs from every well, every ten years,
in this round Hwadang village among the sparse bamboos,
oh, my father
slain under the bayonets.
How could I ever forget that May
with crystal dew foaming on the bamboo-buds?

KIM CHI-HA/김지하

작은 꼬막마저 아사하는
길고 잔인한 여름
하늘도 없는 폭정의 뜨거운 여름이었다
끝끝내
조국의 모든 세월은 황톳길은
우리들의 희망은

낡은 쪽배들 햇볕에 바스라진
뻘길을 지나면 다시 모래밭
희디흰 고랑 너머
청천 드높은 하늘에 갈리든
아아 그날의 만세는 십년을 지나
철삿줄 파고드는 살결에 숨결 속에

너의 목소리를 느끼며 흐느끼며
나는 간다 애비야
네가 죽은 곳
부춧머리 갯가에 숭어가 뛸 때
가마니 속에서 네가 죽은 곳

고 원/KO WON

That was a long and cruel summer,
even babies were starving:
a hot summer of tyranny without heaven.
That summer choked, to the end,
all the time of our nation, yellow dust roads
and our hope altogether.

The fighting call of that day,
passing the muddy beach where the sun battered
the old wooden boats to dust, moving again to wheat paddies,
and then crossing over the bleached furrows,
finally thundered at the clear-blue, high skies.
It's been ten years since, and now the call of that day
comes alive in the breath and flesh, barbed wires piercing.

Feeling your voice, feeling it in my heart,
I am going, Father,
where you died,
where you died, indeed, wrapped in a rice sack
while the trouts were jumping along Pujutmŏri Brook.

KIM CHI-HA/김지하

푸른 옷

새라면 좋겠네
물이라면 혹시는 바람이라면

여윈 알몸을 가둔 옷
푸른 빛이여 바다라면
바다의 한 때나마 꿈일 수나마 있다면

가슴에 꽂히어 아프게 피흐르다
굳어버린 네모의 붉은 표지여 네가 없다면
네가 없다면
아아 죽어도 좋겠네
재되어 흩날리는 운명이라도 나는 좋겠네

캄캄한 밤에 그토록
새벽이 오길 애가 타도록
기다리는 눈들에 흘러넘치는 맑은 눈물들에
영롱한 나팔꽃 한번이나마 어릴 수 있다면
햇살이 빛날 수만 있다면

꿈마다 먹구름 뚫고 열리던 새푸른 하늘
쏟아지는 햇살아래 잠시나마
서 있을 수만 있다면 좋겠네
푸른 옷에 갇힌채 죽더라도 좋겠네

그것이 생시라면
그것이 지금이라면
그것이 끝끝내 끝끝내
가리워지지만 않는다면.

BLUE SUIT

I wish this were a bird,
water, or perhaps the wind.

This suit, confining my body, thin and naked.
Its blue color: I wish it were the sea,
even a glimpse of the sea, a piece of dream.

This square red badge, sticking in my heart,
painfully bleeding, and then clotted.
But for you, only but for you,
oh, I would even be happy to die,
even with a destiny of scattering ashes.

If a lucid morning-glory could dazzle just once
in the eyes so anxiously awaiting dawn
at such a dark night and
in their crystal tears overflowing there,
and if sunbeams could possibly shine;

if I could stand a moment in the sunrays
pouring down from the deep blue sky,
breaking through the black clouds in every dream,
I would die willingly confined in this blue suit.

I wish it were real,
were it right now,
    and the real would never,
      never be covered to the end.

KIM CHI-HA/김지하

아무도 없다

여기서부터
저기까지는
아무도 없다.

검은 개천 위에
달빛이 몰락하는 돌다리 위에
이 이상스럽도록 아름다운
하이얀 입김서린 집속엔
아무도 없다.

캄캄하고
달속을 둔주하는 銀錢에 짓눌려
뒤틀리는 사지의 낡은 꿈속은 캄캄하고

푸르게 물드는
腦속에서 죽어가는 나의
나로부터 길에는 아무도 없다.

NOBODY IS THERE

Nobody at all
from here
to there.

Nobody is there
above a black ditch,
on a stone bridge where moonlight collapses,
and in this strangely beautiful house
steamed white with breaths.

Dark
is the middle of a dream of my
twisting limbs crushed by a silver coin
running round in the moon; it's dark.

And nobody is there
from me to the road,
my Self dying in the brain
which is being dyed blue.

KIM CHI-HA / 김지하

서울

칼이 서는 곳
칼자루 보이지 않는 안개 서린 곳
밤새워 흘린 핏자욱
마저 보이지 않는
대낮에도 시퍼렇게 칼이 서는 곳

휘저어도 휘저어도
잡히지 않는 곳
발 붙일 수 없는 알 수 없는
떠날 수 조차 없는
한번 묻혀 다시는 헤칠 길마저 없는
늪이여 저주의 도시
저 하늘에도 가득히 칼이 서는 곳

행여
너를 이기기 위해
행여 너를 이기기 위해 서울이여
넋은 네 칼날 아래 남김 없이 바쳐졌다
주리고 병들은 빈 육신도 마저
부질없는 반역 속에 불타버렸다

남은 것은 지는 것
남은 마지막 단 한번은 칼날 위에
꽃처럼 붉게 붉게 떨어지는 것
이기기 위해
죽어 너를 끝끝내 이기기 위해
죽어 피로써
네 칼날을 녹슬도록 만들기 위해

고 원/KO WON

SEOUL

A place where the swords stand,
where the hilts are obscured in the thick mist,
where the sharp swords stand even in daylight
hiding the traces of blood
shed throughout the night.

A place which, for all grappling,
no hands can catch;
that is a swamp, an accursed city,
where nobody can set foot or may leave,
a mysterious place from where, once driven in,
no one can find a way out at all.
The swords stand full in that sky.

Wishing
to overcome you,
wishing to overcome you, oh Seoul,
we gave all our souls beneath your blade.
There burnt our starved, sick
and empty bodies in lame revolts.

What is left is to fall down:
for the very last time, on your blade,
oh, on that blade,
falling like a red, red flower
in order to overcome,
to overcome you at last in dying,
to have your blade rust
with our blood in dying.

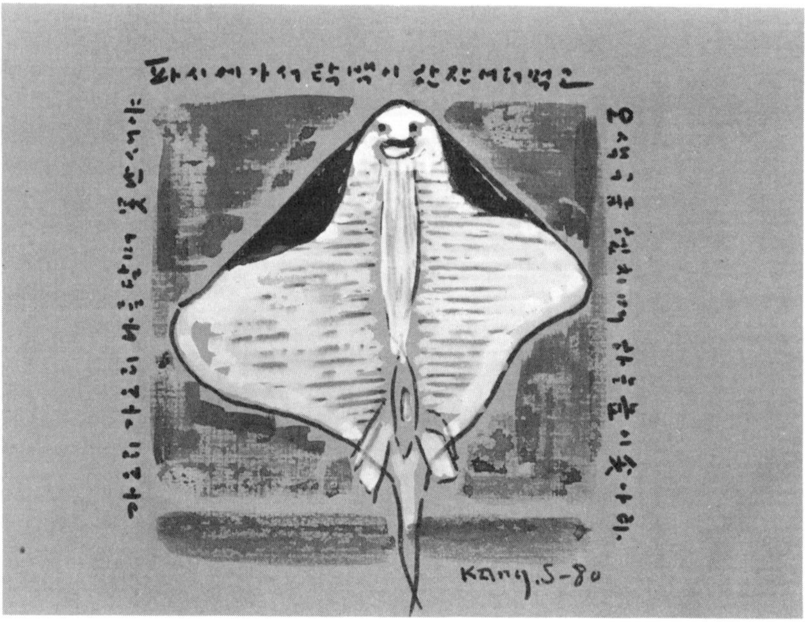
파시에가서 탁백이 한잔 얻어먹고
Kang. 5-80

YANG SŎNG-U
(b. 1943)

Yang first published his poems in 1970 while he was a student of Korean literature at Chonnam University. When he read his poem "The Winter Republic" at a public meeting in 1975, he was dismissed from the girls' high school where he had been teaching. Shortly after he was arrested as a signatory of the 1977 Charter for National Democratic Salvation, the Japanese intellectual monthly *Sekai* published Yang's long poem titled "The Notes of Slaves" in Japanese translation in June of the same year. As a result, new charges were imposed on him and he was imprisoned until the spring of 1979.

Two books of his poetry, *Palsangpŏp* (Expression, 1972) and *Sinhayŏ sinhayŏ* (Oh, Your Vassal, 1974), were followed by another two volumes which came out while he was in jail: *Kyŏul konghwaguk* (The Winter Republic, 1977) and *Noye such'ŏp* (The Notes of Slaves, 1978), the former published in Seoul only to be confiscated, and the latter in Tokyo, Japan. Yang's preoccupation with the people is expressed in his own foreword (originally a note) to *The Winter Republic:* "Even though I can abandon these poems, I cannot abandon this land. Even if I can throw these poems away, I cannot abandon the flesh, language, love, sigh, and tears of my neighbors. Even at the cost of these poems, I must recapture the freedom we were robbed of."

YANG SŎNG-U / 양성우

새

보이지 않는 곳에서 퍼덕이다가
주린 짐승의 과녁으로 쓰러지고
먼지 속에서 죽어
밤새 맺힌 이슬처럼
소리 없이 죽어,
깃털 뽑혀
보이지 않는 곳으로 돌아가는
깨끗한 부리,
끝 모를 허공을 쪼아대며
혹은 잠긴 문틈으로 지저귀다가
가슴 치며 가슴 치며
가는 넋들아.

BIRDS

Fluttering in an unseen place,
    and then falling down
        to be the target of a hungry beast;
dead in dust,
dead without a sound
like a night-long dewdrop;
those clean beaks
returning to an unseen place
with feathers pulled off.
Knocking on the endless skies,
or twittering through the locked doors,
    you, souls, going,
      striking the heart, striking the heart.

YANG SŎNG-U/ 양성우

겨울공화국

여보게 우리들의 논과 밭이 눈을 뜨면서
뜨겁게 뜨겁게 숨쉬는 것을 보았는가
여보게 우리들의 논과 밭이 갈아앉으며
누군가의 이름을 부르는 것을
부르면서 불끈 불끈 주먹을 쥐고
으드득 으드득 이빨을 갈고
헛웃음을 껄껄껄 웃어대거나
웃다가 새하얗게 까무라쳐서
누군가의 발밑에 까무라쳐서
한꺼번에 한꺼번에 죽어가는 것을 보았는가

총과 칼로 사납게 윽박지르고
논과 밭에 자라나는 우리들의 뜻을
군화발로 지근지근 짓밟아대고
밟아대며 조상들을 비웃어대는
지금은 겨울인가
한밤중인가
논과 밭이 얼어 붙는 겨울 한때를
여보게 우리들은 우리들을
무엇으로 달래야 하는가

삼천리는 여전히 살기 좋은가
삼천리는 여전히 비단 같은가
거짓말이다 거짓말이다
날마다 우리들은 모른체하고
다소곳이 거짓말에 귀기울이며
뼈 가르는 채찍질을 견뎌내야 하는
노예다 머슴이다 허수아비다

THE WINTER REPUBLIC

My friend, did you see our paddies and fields,
opening their eyes, take hot, hot breaths?
My friend, did you see them, sinking,
call someone's name,
and calling, clench their fists fast,
grind their teeth vexedly,
burst out a feigned laughter,
and laughing, faint away pale,
swooning beneath someone's feet
and die altogether?

That which threatens harshly with swords and guns,
tramples our wills instilled in these fields
beneath soldiers' boots,
and trampling, laughs at our ancestors—
is it now winter?
the middle of night?
With what, my friend,
shall we comfort ourselves
this winter time when our fields are frozen?

Is the three-thousand-li land still livable?
Is the land still as beautiful as silks?
That's a lie; that is a lie.
We are serfs, scarecrows
lending our ears silently to lies
in a pretense of knowing nothing everyday
and having to tolerate whips that cut our bones.

YANG SŎNG-U/양성우

부끄러워라 부끄러워라 부끄러워라
부끄러워라 잠든 아기의 베개 맡에서
결코 우리는 부끄러울 뿐
한 마디도 떳떳하게 말할 수 없네
물려 줄 것은 부끄러움 뿐
잠든 아기의 베개 맡에서
우리들은 또 무엇을 변명해야 하는가

서로를 날카롭게 노려만 보고
한마디도 깊은 말을 나누지 않고
번쩍이는 칼날을 감추어 두고
언 땅을 조심 조심 스쳐가는구나
어디선가 일어서라 고함질러도
배고프기 때문에 비틀거리는
어지럽지만 머무를 곳이 없는
우리들은 또 어디로 가야 하는가
우리들을 모질게 재갈물려서
짓이기며 짓이기며 내리 모는 자는
누구인가 여보게 그 누구인가
등덜미에 찍혀 있는 우리들의 흉터,
채찍 맞은 우리들의 슬픈 흉터를
바람아 동지 섣달 모진 바람아
네 씁쓸한 칼끝으로도 지울 수 없다

돌아가야 할 것은 돌아가야 하네
담벼랑에 붙어 있는 농담거리도
바보 같은 라디오도 신문 잡지도
저녁이면 멍청하게 장단 맞추는
TV도 지금쯤은 정직해져서
한반도의 책상 끝에 놓여져야 하네

Shame, shame, shame!
We are only shameful
at the bedside of our sleeping children.
Forbidden to say a word fairly,
we have nothing but shame to bequeath them.
What must we say again to defend us
at their bedside?

Exchanging a sharp glare,
sharing no meaningful words,
and hiding a well-sharpened knife, aren't we
carefully passing each other across the frozen land?
Although a voice somewhere calls for our resistance,
we, dizzily staggering from hunger,
have no place to stay for a while;
where can we go from here?
Who is the one who has ruthlessly
put us to the yoke and, trampling, trampling down,
goes on driving us? Who is that, my friend?
You, the wind, the severe wintry wind,
even with the bitter edge of your knife,
cannot sweep away the scars carved on us—
the sad scars of his whip deep in our backs.

My friend, what ought to return must return.
What's the use of jokes hung on the wall,
foolish radios, newspapers, and magazines
and the TV which adjusts its tune
to every evening's vacuousness?
All this should be honest by now
and put on the Peninsula's table.

YANG SŎNG-U / 양성우

비겁한 것들은 사라져 가고
더러운 것들도 사라져 가고
마당에도 골목에도 산과 들에도
사랑하는 것들만 가득히 서서
가슴으로만 가슴으로만 이야기 하고
여보게 화약냄새 풍기는 겨울 벌판에
잡초라도 한줌씩 돋아나야 할 걸세

이럴 때는 모두들 눈물을 닦고
한강도 무등산도 말하게 하고
산새들도 한번쯤 말하게 하고
여보게
우리들이 만일 게으르기 때문에
우리들의 낙인을 지우지 못한다면
차라리 과녁으로 나란히 서서
사나운 자의 총끝에 쓰러지거나
쓰러지며 쓰러지며 부르짖어야 할 걸세

사랑하는 모국어로 부르짖으며
진달래 진달래 진달래들이 언 땅에도
싱싱하게 피어나게 하고
논둑에도 밭둑에도 피어나게 하고
여보게
우리들의 슬픈 겨울을
몇 번이고 몇 번이고 일컫게 하고
묶인 팔다리로 봄을 기다리며
한사코 온 몸을 버둥거려야 하지 않는가
여보게

고 원/KO WON

All the cowards and filth having disappeared
and only beloved ones instead filling up
gardens, lanes, hills, and plains
speak from heart to heart—
that's the way we have to make it.
My friend, we should see even a handful of weeds
growing in each gunpowder-smoking wintry field.

That's the time for all of us to stop weeping,
have the Han River and Mt. Mudŭng speak out
and have mountain birds say a word.
My friend,
if we are too lazy to erase our stigmas,
then our choice will be to line up as targets
and fall to the brutes' guns, and then,
falling, falling, we shall still cry out.

Crying out in our own dear language,
why don't we make azaleas, azaleas, azaleas
come alive and bloom out of this frozen land,
blooming all over the paddies?
My friend,
why don't we have our sad winter
spoken of, time and time again?
And mustn't we, shackled tight, struggle on
to the last, while waiting for the spring,
my friend?

YANG SŎNG-U/양성우

夏日有感

그대 휘두르는 칼, 닳아서 굽을 때까지
나무는 산에서 졸고만 있다더냐.
그대 마시는 술, 이웃의 한숨이
으슥한 골짜기를 채울 때까지
바위는 비탈에서 졸고만 있다더냐.
그대 무너져,
발 구르며 안타깝게 젖을 때까지
풀잎은 벌판에서
시들고만 있다더냐.
그대 불 같이 잔인해
그대 불 같이 잔인해
죽은 자를 또다시 죽일지라도
우리, 숨어서
쫓기고만 있다더냐.

ON A SUMMER DAY

How would trees only keep dozing in mountains
till the sword you wield turns worn and bent?
How would rocks simply be sleeping at slopes
till the drink you indulge, that is,
neighbor's sigh, fills up secluded valleys?
How would grass leaves
only grow withered in wilderness
till you, crumbled at last,
painfully howl, stamping?
How can we possibly, still hiding,
just keep being chased
despite you, spiteful,
brutal as fire,
kill the killed once again?

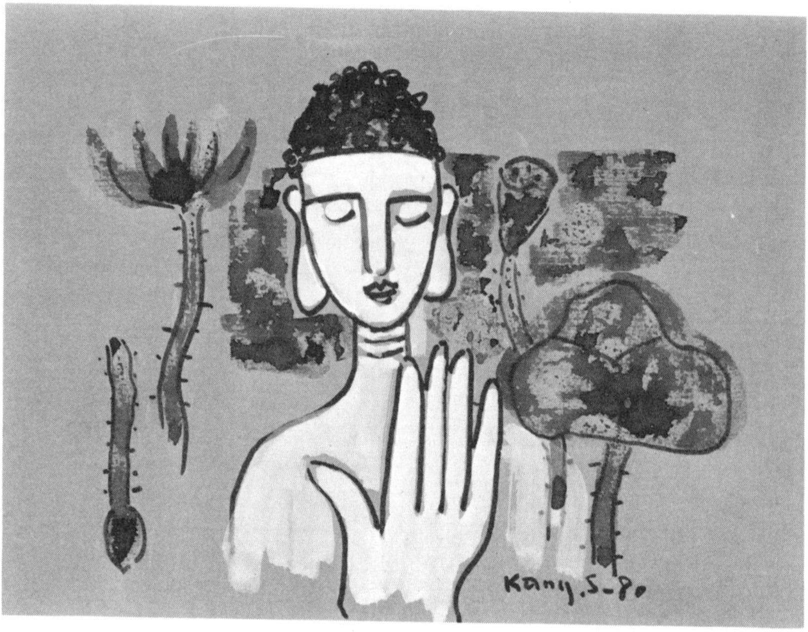
Kang.S-80

KO ŬN
(b. 1933)

Ko Ŭn spent twelve years of his youth as a Buddhist monk until he renounced the priesthood in 1963. His literary career began in 1958 with his numerous publications, including short stories and essays as well as poetry, the latest volumes of which are *Ipsan* (Entering the Priesthood, 1977) and *Saebyŏk-kil* (An Early Morning Road, 1978). The three poems translated here are selected from the latter. In 1974, he joined the Writers' Association for the Practice of Freedom in Seoul and has been active (formerly as its president) in matters related to human rights and democracy in general and workers' rights in particular. After having been harassed and arrested by the police and the Korean Central Intelligence Agency several times, he is—as of August 1980—facing military trial for an alleged connection with the popular uprising of Kwangju (a southwestern city of South Korea) which took place in May, 1980. "I believe," says he in the Afterword to his latest book, "that I must turn the poetry I write into everybody's poetry. I want my readers to read these poems amending whatever is bad. That is my true wish."

KO ŬN/고 은

푸른 하늘

오 푸른 하늘
그냥 하늘이 아니라
우리 몸뚱이 능지처참의 아픔이로다
그냥 사오천년 안쏟아지는 하늘이 아니라
오늘 원한풀이 못한 우리한테
가슴 벅찬 아픔의 부자로다
오 푸른 하늘
쌍눈 부릅뜨며 우리가 하늘임을 흐느끼게 하는
남북 몇천만 한 겨레의 아픔이로다
푸른 하늘에 내가 있다고 흐느끼게 하는
고려땅 방방곡곡 꽉 찬 아픔이로다

고 원/KO WON

THE BLUE SKY

Oh, the blue sky
is not simply the air, but the pain
of our bodies hacked to pieces.
Not the sky sustaining for thousands of years
but to us, unable to vent our spite,
it is an expanse of heartrending pain.
Oh, the blue sky: that is the pain
of the whole nation, north and south in one,
feeling poignantly that we are the heaven;
the pain filling every corner of the land of Koryŏ,
feeling my Self standing in the middle of the azure.

KO ŬN/고 은

화살

우리 모두 화살이 되어
온몸으로 가자
허공 뚫고
온몸으로 가자
가서는 돌아오지 말자
박혀서
박힌 아픔과 함께 썩어서 돌아오지 말자

우리 모두 숨 끊고 활시위를 떠나자
몇 십년 동안 가진 것
몇 십년 동안 누린 것
몇 십년 동안 쌓은 것
행복이라던가
뭣이라던가
그런 것 다 넝마로 버리고
화살이 되어 온몸으로 가자

허공이 소리친다
허공 뚫고
온몸으로 가자
저 캄캄한 대낮 과녁이 달려온다
이윽고 과녁이 피 뿜으며 쓰러질 때
단 한번
우리 모두 화살로 피를 흘리자

돌아오지 말자
돌아오지 말자

오 화살 정의의 병사여 영령이여

ARROWS

Let us all become an arrow
and go with our entire body.
Piercing the empty air,
let's go with our whole being.
Let's go and never return.
Stuck and rotten with the pain
of being stuck, let's not return.

With bated breath, let us all
jump out of the bow string.
Doing away with what we, for many years,
have been having, what we have enjoyed,
what we have saved, things like happiness
and the like, all junk,
let's go as an arrow.

The empty air is calling us.
Piercing it through,
let's go with our entire body.
The target is approaching in that dark daytime.
When the target finally collapses, bleeding,
let us, only once,
shed blood ourselves as an arrow.

Let's not return.
Let's not return.

Oh arrows, just soldiers, great spirits!

KO ŬN/고 은

고향

이미 우리에게는
태어난 곳이 고향이 아니다
자란 곳이 고향이 아니다
산과 들 달려오는
우리 역사가 고향이다

그리하여 바람찬 날
우리가 쓰러질 곳
그곳이 고향이다

우리여 우리여
모두 다 그 고향으로 가자
어머니가 기다린다
어머니인 역사가 기다린다
그 고향으로 가자

HOME

To us, already,
a birthplace is no longer our home.
The place we were brought up is not either.
Our history, rushing to us
through fields and hills, is our home.

Home for us is, then,
a place where we shall die
willingly, on a stormy day.

Why don't we—say, *we*—
all of us, go to that home?
Our mother is waiting for us.
Our motherly history is waiting.
Let's go to that home.

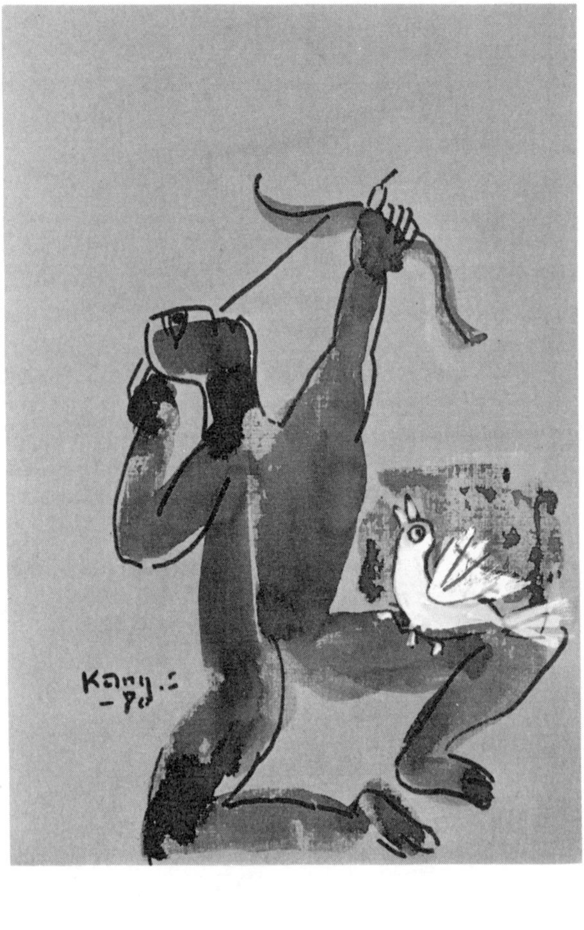

KO WON
(b. 1925)

Ko Won studied literature in Korea and England before he came to the United States in 1964. He continued his studies at the University of Iowa Writers' Workshop, graduating with an M.F.A., and New York University, where he earned his Ph. D. in Comparative Literature. He has taught at colleges and universities in Seoul and New York. His publications include seven volumes of poetry written in Korean, the latest of which are *Mirunamu* (Poplar, 1976) and *Puksori-e t'anŭn pyŏl* (Stars Burning in Tune to the Sound of Drums, 1979), both published in New York; *Contemporary Korean Poetry,* an anthology of his translations (Iowa, 1970); *The Turn of Zero,* a book of English poems (Merrick, N.Y., 1974); *Buddhist Elements in Dada* (New York, 1977); *Kalmaegi* (Seagulls), a collection of miscellaneous essays (Tokyo, 1979). Winner of the Kansas City Star Award in Poetry (1966), he has published English poems, articles, and translations in many magazines and journals. Besides teaching, writing, and translating, he has been actively engaged in support of the imprisoned Korean poets and writers.

KO WON/고 원

탈상의 날에

가난한 탈상의 제단입니다만
굽어보시는 여덟분의
신주가 온통 조국만합니다.
〈인민혁명당〉 희생자
하나 하나 성함을 부르면서
우리 다 같이 분향 재배합니다.

짓밟히며 살아남은
당신들의 혈육 형제 자매가 여기
향에 돌려서 바치는 술은
원통하고 분한 눈물입니다.
가슴이 터지게 원통하고 분해서
혁명을 약속하는 피가 고였읍니다.

죄를 꾸며 뒤집어씌우고는
당신들의 목을 조르다니요.
목을 조르고는 불에 태우다니요.
그 원수를 찾아 나서야지요.

오늘은 우리가 상복을 완전히
전투복으로 갈아입는 날.
4월 9일에 사무친 곡소리를
승리의 노래로 바꾸기 위해서
교수대를 향해 달려가야지요.

당신들의 마음이 진달래가 된
우리 4월이 정녕 영광스럽게
절 한번 더 올리고 어서 가겠읍니다.

GOING OUT OF MOURNING

What a poor altar for the last mourning, but
as big as the whole country is the substance
of the tablets, eight of you looking around at us.
Calling each name of the "People's Revolutionary
Party" victims, we burn incense and bow twice to each.

The wine offered by the trampled survivors—
your brothers and sisters, flesh and blood—
circling cups in the incense smoke,
is our tears of regret and wrath.
Full of pained resentment,
there stagnates blood of a promised revolution.

How could they lay a fabricated guilt on you
and dare strangle you to death?
How could they burn your strangled bodies away?
We must go out in search of the enemies.

Today we are changing completely
our mourning dress to fighting clothes.
To turn the wailing voice which struck out
on that April ninth into a song of victory,
we should rush toward the gallows.

We will go ahead right after bowing once more
to honor a real glory to the April that is ours,
in which your hearts have bloomed to azaleas.

KO WON/고 원

어머니

어머니
어머니, 당신은
당신의 아들이 제 몸을 태워
야수를 향해 항쟁의 불을 지른
바로 그 불길입니다.

모든 노동자들이 당신을
노동자의 어머니로 받드는 까닭은
빼앗겨 굶주린 창자에
불 타는 젖을 주시기 때문입니다.
당신의 품, 불 속에 안겨서
끝까지 같이 타고 싶기 때문입니다.

당신은 저 더러운 서울 청계천
평화시장의 어머니만이 아닙니다.
싸워서 이룩할 평화의 어머니지요.
당신이 갇혀있는 감옥을 헐고
남북의 담을 헐었을 때
당신은 또 통일의 어머니가 될 것입니다.

우리 어머니, 이소선선생,
우리는 이리를 앞두고 날마다
이
솟은
이를 갑니다.
톱니를 갈고 칼을 갑니다.
그럴 때마다 불이 튑니다.

고 원/KO WON

MOTHER

Mother,
Mother, you are
the flame itself which blazed out
when your son, by burning himself,
set fight on fire against wild beasts.

We, all workers, honor you
as a *worker's mother,* because
you feed our exploited, starving stomachs
with your burning milk, and we, nestling
in your bosom, that is, in the fire,
want to burn together, to the last.

You are not just the mother of Peace Market
along that filthy *Clean Ditch* section of Seoul;
you are the mother of peace to be won by us.
With the prison you are locked in pulled down
and the South-North wall finally demolished,
you will also be the mother of unification.

Our mother, Madam Yi So-sŏn,
say, we, facing the wolves,
grind our teeth
    risen high
    with much vexation,
and sharpen cogwheels and knives everyday.
Flames flash from there each time.

KO WON/고 원

아아 어머니,
지금도 속에서 자꾸 불이 나네요.
태일이 재에서 불길이 솟네요.
그래서 이소선과 아들딸들은
먹지 않고도 참 억세게 살 수 있네요.
어머니 불빛으로 어둠을 쏘면서
어머니와 아들딸들은 참 불처럼 사랑하네요.

우리 어머니, 노동자의 어머니,
배고픈 창자에 한모금 더 불을 주십시오.
그래서 끝까지 같이 강산에 탑시다.
이글이글 우리들이 타면서
이리떼를 불사릅시다.
태일이의 원수,
노동자의 원수,
민족의 원수를 태워버립시다.

고 원/KO WON

Ah, Mother, you see,
our hearts flare up again at this moment.
The fire jumps up out of T'aeil's ashes.
So, Yi So-sŏn and sons and daughters
can live stoutly, for sure, without eating.
Mother's light shooting at the dark,
the spark of love kindles mother and children.

Our mother, worker's mother,
now pour one more draught of fire
into our hungry stomachs—so that we burn
together to the end, all over the land.
Ourselves aflame, aglow,
        let us throw
     the flocked wolves to blazes.
Let us destroy and reduce to ashes
   T'aeil's enemy,
     worker's enemy,
        the enemy of our nation.

KO WON/고 원

아직도 숨을 쉰다면

외로운 것이 아니다.
인기척 없이
총칼 총총
총의 밀림에 갇혀서
아직도 숨을 쉰다면
외로운 것은 아니다.

시간마저 죽어가는 잠시.
별이 총총 애타는 하늘은
맘 속에서만 밝은 자리.
아직도 숨을 쉰다면 외롭지 않다.
치가 떨려 치욕을 깨물면서
어둠의 무게를 등으로 떠받치는
가쁜 호흡이 고독은 아니다.

그러면 또 기다림일까.
남쪽 혼을 붙들고
밀림 서울에 새벽을 기다림일까.

저 짐승 새끼 어깨에 박힌
저것을 잡아라.
높은 빛을 가릴만큼 크게
화약으로 만든 미친 별들—
    저 별을 잡아라.

고 원/KO WON

IF YOU ARE STILL BREATHING

It's not loneliness.
Locked in a gun jungle—
swarms of swords and guns—with no
signs of people's presence,
you are not lonely
if you are still breathing.

A while when even time is dying;
where the impatient sky, full of stars,
is only bright in your hearts.
Still breathing, you are not lonely.
Indignant, biting back at humiliation,
your backs propping against the weight
of darkness, hard breathing is not isolation.

Is this then to wait again?
Holding the southern soul,
wait for the dawn for the jungle Seoul?

Catch those things nailed on that
son-of-a-bitch's shoulders!
Crazy stars made of gunpowder
big enough to block light on high—
    catch the stars!

ABOUT THE ARTIST

Kang Sin Suk (Chungbuk, Korea, 1913), son of a leading patriot who fought in China for Korea's independence during World War II, has taught fine art at Harbin Industrial College (Manchuria, 1945), Dong-a University (Pusan, Korea, 1967), and Milan College of Technology (Italy, 1978). He also served the South Korean government as Director of the Bureau of Decoration (1948) and was a wartime artist affiliated with the South Korean Navy (1952). The exhibitions of his art work include those in Seoul (1953, 1977), Milan (1978), and Paris (1979). Mr. Kang has been living in New York since 1979.

Typeset by Merrick Typographers (Merrick, N.Y.). Printed by Mill River Press (Brooklyn, N.Y.).

R0147086835 HUM

895.
7108
S726

HOUSTON PUBLIC LIBRARY

CENTRAL LIBRARY
500 MCKINNEY